PRAISE

"Elizabeth Onyeabor has written a must-read poetry collection for anyone who has lived, despaired, loved, and hoped. Read this book slowly, poem by poem, and get inspired by a woman whose writing bounces easily between life's existential depths and playfulness."

—ERICA APPELROS, Associate Professor in Philosophy of Religion, Lund University, Sweden (www.appelroscoaching.se)

"I thoroughly enjoyed and could relate to so many of Elizabeth's poems. I found myself standing between Love and Fear as she did in her poem, I Call Myself. My heart ached as she shared the traumatic moments of Mother Protector. I pulled back into my safe cocoon in her poem, Who Am I? I returned to my childhood courage and sense of adventure in her poem, Effortlessly. If you love writing that is authentic, true, and healing, I encourage you to add this poetry collection to your bookshelf."

—STEVE GARVIN, The Story Architect, Gifts Into Gold (www.giftsintogold.com), and author of *Arrived: How Facing the Darkness Inspired Me to Shine*

"Elizabeth is such a talented woman. *Escaping the Shadows* spoke to me on so many levels. If you've experienced a loss, tragedy, and need resilience and acceptance, you'll love this collection of poems. Together with the acceptance of grief, Elizabeth shares her journey in a way that is both touching and inspirational."

—BREANNA GUNN, CEO, Breanna Gunn Enterprises (www.breannagunn.com)

ESCAPING THE SHADOWS

OTHER BOOKS BY ELIZABETH

From the Shadows: A Journey of Self-Discovery and Renewal
(Sojourn Publishing)

The Light Within: Freedom Through Forgiveness
(Achara Bambus Creative Works)

Elizabeth Onyeabor books are available for order through Amazon.com and other retailers.

My Gift to You

Deepen your experience with
The Light Within: Practice Guide and visualization recordings.

*3 Keys to Feel Good Enough:
A 30-Day Guide for a More Joyful You*
(Achara Bambus Creative Works)
Free ebook

Available only at www.ElizabethOnyeabor.com/gifts

ESCAPING THE SHADOWS

A Pilgrimage with Poetry

Elizabeth Onyeabor

Escaping the Shadows: A Pilgrimage with Poetry
Copyright © 2021 Elizabeth Onyeabor.
Achara Bambus Creative Works, LLC
All rights reserved.

Book cover design by Elizabeth Onyeabor and Debbie O'Byrne (www.jetlaunch.net)
Cover photo: Shaunda Whitworth
Angels and Demons poem co-created with Kristine Giles
Editing by Eye Comb Editors, LLC (www.eyecombeditors.com) and Lucid Design Studios (www.luciddesignstudios.com)

No part of this book may be reproduced, stored in a retrieval system, or transmitted, in any form or by any means—electronic, mechanical, photocopying, recording, or otherwise—without the author's prior written permission. The only exception is by a reviewer, who may quote short excerpts in a review with appropriate citations.

Elizabeth Onyeabor books are available for order through Amazon.com and other retailers.

Visit my website for gifts.
www.elizabethonyeabor.com/gifts

Connect with me on social media.
LinkedIn: www.linkedin.com/in/elizabethonyeabor
Twitter: www.twitter.com/efonyeabor
Instagram: www.instagram.com/elizabethonyeabor
Facebook: www.facebook.com/elizabethonyeaborauthor

First Printing: July 2021.
Publisher: Achara Bambus Creative Works, LLC
ISBN-13: 978-1955681025 (paperback)
ISBN 13: 978-1955681032 (digital)

Printed in the United States of America.

DEDICATION

For Gillis, who aided and abetted exodus from the shadows

CONTENTS

INTRODUCTION — 1
BUBBLES BURST — 3

Breezing — 6
Technology Will Not — 7
God's Handiwork — 8
Dolphin and Dove — 9
Touching Tempos — 11
Beloved — 13
Amore — 14
Entwining — 15
Expandable — 16
Persnickity Passion — 17
Void — 18
Bed of Thorns — 19
Poison — 20
Smarts — 21
Remembering You — 22
Absence — 23
Meandering Mind — 24
Depression — 25
Am I Worthy? — 27
Buts — 28
Maybe — 29
Argumental — 30
Is It Fear? — 31

Timeless	33
Stormed	34
GUARDIANS OF GRIEF	**35**
Doomed	38
The Secret	39
Cockled Bluebells	41
Shattered	42
Shaming Tree	44
Pathways	46
Bliss Amiss	47
Vulnerability	48
Caged Bird	49
Faces	50
Indecision	51
A Shadowy Friend	52
Who Am I?	53
Angels and Demons	54
Belated Grief	55
Thief	57
Failure	58
Diving	59
Bullish Surrender	60
FINDING FOOTING	**61**
Growth Cycle	64
Blockages	65
Lap Lessons	66
Adventureland	67
Escaping the Shadows	68

Excitement	70
Knowing	71
Mindful	72
Never	73
Rainbow Resonance	74
Warring Heart	75
Sunflowers	76
Seeds of Love	77
Appreciation	78
In the Moment	79
Effortlessly	81
Go Go Go	83
No More Running	84
Connected Again	85
Flow	87
Potential	88
Cleansing Soul	89
Depth Decision	90
Imprisoned	91
Breathing Life	92
HEARTFELT HEALING	**93**
River Flow	96
Mother Protector	98
Watery Wonders	99
Thinking in Ink	100
Penned Flight	101
Heart's Desire	102
Musical Movement	103

Inner Universe	104
Ageless	105
O'er-runneth	106
Springtime Sprouts	108
Chrysalis	109
Resurrection	110
Soul Searching	111
My Body	112
Alignment	113
Traumatic Growth	114
Fear Versus Love	115
Soul Sister	116
Family Prayer	118
Soulmate Dance	119
Solitude	120
Great Day	121
I Call Myself	123
Contentment	124
Serenity	125
Seven Life Lessons	126
ABOUT THE AUTHOR	**129**

INTRODUCTION

Poetry saved me. Between 2012 and 2015, I often longed to sleep forever as an escape from heartache, self-deprecation, and hopelessness. In short, my struggle with severe depression.

Much to my surprise, expression I unintentionally imprisoned over four decades broke out with emancipated rhyme and verse, soothing the outer reaches of my inner ache.

This collection represents the ups and downs and backs and forths of my trek. It spans the times when despair nearly destroyed me to anguishing over losses both authentic and imagined, to unearthing the origins of my agony, and, ultimately, to discovering a lasting way to soothe my soul.

BUBBLES BURST

"I fall apart"

Escaping the Shadows

DIGITAL DELIGHT

morning greeting
shimmering screen

new mail
new message
new comment
new tag

connected
ones and
zeros
binary
unitary
in my
solitary

daily anticipation
digital delight

Elizabeth Onyeabor

BREEZING

gently stirring
hair wisping
lace fluttering
feathery tickling
body caressing
cool whispering
airy soothing
zephyr calming
heat releasing
breezing

TECHNOLOGY WILL NOT

hold your hand
wipe away tears
kiss your cheek
envelop you in its arms
mourn your passing

Elizabeth Onyeabor

GOD'S HANDIWORK

thin threads
twist and turn
left and right
up and down

single strands
lost in life's loops
weaving ways
days upon days

united one by one

into a tapestry by design

DOLPHIN AND DOVE

dolphin and dove
fell deeply in love

dolphin tied wings;
he needed those things

never felt grace
in air like his place

wary of squawk
taloned eagle, hawk

flocking inured
for his family endured

roused to move back
fix what's outta whack

dove eased into sea
no difficulty

swimmingly well
fin and feathers' tale

the pressure of depth
bore down on her health

longed for skyward flight
from this watery bight

Elizabeth Onyeabor

a mourned decision
with inner derision

clarity knew
just what to do

create a way
both to and fro stay

in air and at sea
with ease and feel free

betwixt and between
balanced at last
in life's dream

TOUCHING TEMPOS

I trace along
the downy edge
of face and scalp
tickled by wispy strands

twinkles light
your warm, cocoa eyes
curving at lid's edge
no hint of the crow

curled licorice-black lashes
framed in dramatic arches
relaxing from
their oft-expressive state

a subtle slope savors
gliding gently around
a golden pearl tip
to a broad base

ivory patterns formed
by heredity and handling
bordered within dusty rouge
your infectious smile
spreads to me

Elizabeth Onyeabor

tanned splendor radiates
from your cheek bones
ebony tendrils spiral
kinks above your lobes

soft exhales
a musky metronome
your faint fragrance unique

hearts pulsing in
touching tempos
as if you were here

BELOVED

beloved as autumn's leafy array
beloved as winter's dancing flakes
beloved as spring's newborn life
beloved as summer's sweet rains
beloved as a rose's perfumed petals
beloved as the sun's beaming kiss
beloved as a kitty's contented purr
beloved as a puppy's loyal wag
beloved as a baby's contagious coo
beloved as your face's tender smile
beloved is our love's soft embrace

Elizabeth Onyeabor

AMORE

give me more
of what I search for
open the door
pick me up off the floor
reject horrid self-lore
and deeds past abhor
don't want any more
so take this awful gore
make the mirror j'ta dore
when reflecting
ever more

ENTWINING

bodily
longing
blending
conjoining
enveloping

implausible

mindfully
desiring
co-relating
mooring
entwining

conceivable

Elizabeth Onyeabor

EXPANDABLE

quizzical
the
physical
irresistible
the delectable
distasteful the calisthenical
expandable the abdominal
unwearable
my
apparel

PERSNICKITY PASSION

said she never met me
but showed herself in others

came to believe she was always
on someone else's path to follow

so she kept hidden and
I lived a life resigned

though I thought it would be nice
to feel like others did

she was particularly persnickety
reclusive elusive life's passion

Elizabeth Onyeabor

VOID

gnawing at my bones
feeds fears
breeds foreboding

I am and never will be good enough for lasting love within

foul taunting stench
decomposing banquet
neither nourishes nor satisfies

push harder. join the clean plate club

leftover ideas
morsels of malaise
charred contempt

do more. stop playing with your food

stress-baked toxins
lay passion waste
slaughterhouse soul

worn down by the daily grind

a carousel ride
not making merry
just round and round

there, I said it
not merry

BED OF THORNS

when I lay me down to sleep
I pray tonight I will not weep

inner switch turns
emotion churns

mantle I make
keeps me awake

souls blend as one
fear it undone

grieving runs deep
dreams did not keep

this bed of thorns without a rose
awakens deepest, slumbered prose

Elizabeth Onyeabor

POISON

swallowing
poisoned words

damming
inner whine

rambling
hang over

SMARTS

acronyms follow the name
declaring competency
shouting intelligence
muting what smarts

Elizabeth Onyeabor

REMEMBERING YOU

soft scoops of red ochre
covering your chest

ever-present mound of
heaping emptiness

tamps away the past
wishing you yet breathe

cherished moments rise
calming heartache

fragrant flowers linger
smelling of nostalgia

ABSENCE

absence
makes the heart
fonder
but the mind
wander

drama subsides
unspoken besides

options

stand on our
own

seeds long ago
sown

rich, red soil
transplanted toil

wistful
wishes away
a temporary
stay

heart called me here
now beckons me there

preserve
through my
thoughts
feed flowerbed
plots

Elizabeth Onyeabor

MEANDERING MIND

still house
but not my thoughts
fan swishes round
like my notions

form the words
so many ramblings
not the right time
trip over phrases

sometimes unkind
tightened tongue
better wait
for mad moments' passage

sometimes exacting
even though truth
from my view
is not absolute
connecting dots within
a meandering mind
imperfect pathways
all trees no forest

Escaping the Shadows

DEPRESSION

repression
of expression
begets elimination
of elusive elation

a lone sensation
from inner argumentation
a shaming conflagration
sparked by rumination
a devilish fixation
of my creation

mountains of frustration
abysmal contemplation
an infinite obsession
with hopeless imperfection

seek exhilaration
find no resolution
and this self-suppression
breeds misconception
of infertile passions
in perpetuation

familial desperation
espousing core distortion
of motherly transgression

Elizabeth Onyeabor

a pestering perception
and damning culmination
of myself to shun

AM I WORTHY?

a seed planted

nurtured

grows

it doesn't wonder

about its

worth

Elizabeth Onyeabor

BUTS

claims
betrayed
but
stayed

speaks
enraged
but
stayed

threatens
estranged
but
stayed

MAYBE

maybe it'll be today
maybe morrow he'll go away
maybe we don't mean what we say
maybe that's why we delay
maybe hearts beg to allay
maybe we'll work out a way
maybe we'd sooner stay

Elizabeth Onyeabor

ARGUMENTAL

a tit for tat
I want no blame
but rancored minds
mete the same

you punish me
I punish you
nobody wins
when we are through

we never leave
but what we say
just sends us far
so far away

IS IT FEAR?

is it fear
propelling me
to pursue options
nowhere near
our new home my dear?

is it love
I act from
embolden to seek
for my very own?

what do I want?

I ask myself
questions questions
answers gaunt

how do I balance
what's his and mine?

is it selfish
to pursue
passion and drive
I thought I once had?

why compelled?
why not relax?

enjoy the ride
creeping on this path

Elizabeth Onyeabor

eventually, will I get there?

where will that be?

will I like it?

go with the flow
they say
don't struggle, relax

is it effort?

pursuing options
a rudder to navigate
the stream

can I do the same
for yet another year?
stave off my thoughts,
live around fear?

routine discomfort,
exhausted to change

afraid my talents
won't be enough

what if true to myself is
the bottom line?
will all else fall in place
and be fine?

TIMELESS

love
and
grief
hold hands
around the clock

Elizabeth Onyeabor

STORMED

winds of worry crash astern
I reel off-keel and find I veer
toward an endless hopeless horizon

an imperfect voyage
meets a perfection storm

I grip tighter the helm
though severed from its rudder

a frail figurehead of my own vessel

mental mutiny capsizes with no captain
into a yawning abyss

my craft drifts aimless down
and splinters in blind sea

on the bottom-most bed
anchored by anxiety
I fall apart

GUARDIANS OF GRIEF

"I wailed wretched about what might have been"

KNOTTED NECKLACE

dangling autumn leaves
strung slender on the bough
twain we wither
under life's shady deceit

creaking limbs complain
under mounting fruitlessness
roots a ravished filly
bound by blight

saddled with rowdy self-judgment
I tether my knotted necklace

broody mare beneath
snorts and stomps
awaiting a riderless spurt

middle of the woebegone road
nowhere left to go
giddyup!

rope, make me dance
and swing to silence
as I fall

Elizabeth Onyeabor

DOOMED

a wee me perches on
the porcelain edge to pee

a skull and bony hand
threaten to seize and suck me
into a cesspool

squeezing my eyes tight as a Tupperware lid
flushes the figments away
for today

for tomorrow
a mature me writhes beneath the weight
of a poltergeist pregnant with privy obsessions

slicing razors of regret along my spine
splattering crimson criticisms

with a mouth as deep as the Mariana trench
swallowing me whole

THE SECRET

my turn
to straddle the
black leather seat

careful on my climb
to avoid the
scorching exhaust

chrome and mirrors
reflect leaves, grass
and his raven mustache

a twist of the wrist
a kick of the foot
a rumble of the motor

wind tussles my honey-colored hair

my play dress skirts the surface
as we corner the road
I grip his waist
to stay astride

something crushes my chest

long after
I scramble off
my ribs still squeeze
accordion breaths

Elizabeth Onyeabor

but the motorcycle's not to blame

my body knows
what my mind conceals
for forty-eight years

then, I relive
how

his elbow crushed my chest
and how

his hairy hands snatched my white panties
and how

his raven mustache made me swear to keep
the secret

COCKLED BLUEBELLS

cockleshells,
bluebells
I'm no maid
of these

poppies peal to me

black circles
clang a past
yet to pluck

peachy petals
ring a face
staying the wilds

wilt a dingdong deflower?

mid-life malady
tolls his
dirty deed

while nurture
chimes childish
innocence

forgive a man neighborly

jingle cockles
within my heart
not bluebells
in the dark

Elizabeth Onyeabor

SHATTERED

raised voices
'round a crystal cup

my conscious choice
to move it out of reach
then back again

figuring I was ready
for any crescendo

I was wrong

glass shattered
into ancient arguments
across our kitchen floor

I was not surprised

I swept up shards
of what had been

when the front door
slammed shut
behind him

hope shattered
into fetal fragments
across our kitchen floor

Escaping the Shadows

I wailed wretched
about what might have been

but couldn't sweep up
my brokenness

Elizabeth Onyeabor

SHAMING TREE

bloodied yoke of shame
sooty roots of blame

buried with my name
actions can't reframe

victims all the same

blooms in Guiltyland
sinking blues quicksand

rings a grieving band
knotting gnarled hand

secrets cannot stand

a past loathed to see
shatters what could be

from my shaming tree
maybe hang from thee
kill the pain swiftly

but another way
she suggests today

worked in her own fray
blew quicksand away

brought her where love may

face the pain down deep
roots from which they seep

Escaping the Shadows

dig the tangled heap
clear them as you weep

rout them from your keep

Elizabeth Onyeabor

PATHWAYS

I stand insignificant to
the passageway of possibilities

deeds my heart beckons me toward
mocking laughter echoes dissent
reminds me I can't-shan't-won't

road bumps insurmountable
stumbling blocks barricade progress
flaunt failure where feats should be

small strides toward imagination
knows no limit of can't-shan't-won't
instead paves a can-shall-will
pathway of probabilities

that's the vision I crave
in the signs ahead of me

BLISS AMISS

when mood's amiss
eyes close to dismiss

whatever makes me so blue
wishing past a different view

it's in the how
focus on now

pick a pleasant sound
anything from around

plumed pigeon coos
cream canary woos

whispers the dove
inside echoes love

free to fly on my wings
focus not on external things

climb on, perch upon my back
there's nothing within you lack

the world is yours, draw in deep
these thoughts always to keep

feathery tingles roost
nesting an inner boost

Elizabeth Onyeabor

VULNERABILITY

soft bellied button
my darling pushes
every six months
a clockwork crisis

I jab
dissolution looms

other knobs gnaw
insecurity
new, foreign city
chaos, criminality

I fret
kidnapper prowls

fixed-term contract expiring
loyalty lacks as the
time bomb ticks

I hunt
competition mounts

partner
place
position

I watch
commitment
tick to
zero

CAGED BIRD

flap and flop
around and back

sometimes in circles
sometimes not

wistful wings beat
beyond metal mesh

but know no escape

feathers of futility
swing in feigned flight

sweet songs suffer silence
while the wicked warbles

pity poor Polly's gilded jail
oblivious it's my own

Elizabeth Onyeabor

FACES

beneath a sham serenity
howling whirlwinds mask pleas

sidelined selves seek synergy
"I love you"
"Blend with me"
"We are one"

but the eye of her storm
has no ears

INDECISION

arbitrary deadlines
for my decision

stay or go
where from here

imagining happy aloneness
wherever I am

choose how to feel
focus on shade or sun

struggle
to grasp joy now

smothered
or just cocooning

Elizabeth Onyeabor

A SHADOWY FRIEND

because of inner enmity
you suffered when alone

because I masked our guilt and shame
you shunned me with your might

because you shaped a stalker
you knew me dark and scary

because you assimilate my ache
you grow in compassion

because I haunt you no more
you gain a certain peace

because we dance in duality
you no more air disgrace

because I'm ever present
you watch me from the light

because I love you so
you never stay alone

WHO AM I?

I wonder
who am I?

I shrink from the spectacle
magnified by a thousand faults

too fat too stupid too whatever

and a skin-and-bone self-worth
starving like a scorned refugee

who am I?

when can I
look through untainted lens or
resettle sated in my motherland?

who am I?

when can a blurry heart see clear
and compassion grow ears?

will I ever fill my soul
I wonder
with
who I am?

Elizabeth Onyeabor

ANGELS AND DEMONS

demons in my head
want me dead

angels in my mind
sing I'm fine

BELATED GRIEF

your face shone
in a plastic way
formaldehyde, I imagine
it's just your shell
I turned away
it's not you anymore
why did I want to look, anyway?

I said my goodbyes
we knew this day would come
I don't need to part this way

we talked by phone
I read my tribute
how smells of sawdust
give me fondest thoughts
only of you and what you built
but more than homes and buildings
you gave us a foundation for life

didn't we three say farewell?
didn't I tell you I love you?
didn't you say the same?

why so strong an ache
more than one year since
we put you two in
your final resting places?

Elizabeth Onyeabor

didn't I let go?
did I suppress again?
this intense longing
I never fully allowed
myself to feel your loss

now, more than one year hence
I finally, truly, grieve

THIEF

death's

a

thief

steals
love
and
brings
grief

Elizabeth Onyeabor

FAILURE

fear to fail,
fail to act
stagnant
cycle
repeats

fear to fail,
fail to act
prophecy
complete

DIVING

troubles tumble
along the precipice
shaking loose foundations

gargoyles gather
in an avalanche of anxieties
eroding inmost grounding

screams suffocate
the stillness with echoes
encircling the chasm

agate arms
abut bedrock bosoms

embracing my swan dive

Elizabeth Onyeabor

BULLISH SURRENDER

relentless in my red-caped fight
a snort a stomp a charge
no spear no sword
tramples
the beast of my burdens

kicking up dusty defiance
dumping bullshit in my bowels

some bullies deserve to die

a horn in each hand wrests
a twist a turn a charge
of my life
tender juices dribble down the jaw
sweet meat
of my surrender

FINDING FOOTING

"A pilgrimage to pacify"

SKIING

a frozen flight
on solid waters
gliding swooshing winding
on powdery blue-white sheets
a tethered bird slaloming

Elizabeth Onyeabor

GROWTH CYCLE

deeply rooted
tapping sustenance
growing, sprouting
trunk and limb
budding, blossoming

summer's verdant green
falling into orange-red
then naked, paralyzing winter
frozen in an icy desert

budding blossoming
trunk and limb
growing, sprouting
tapping sustenance
deeply rooted

BLOCKAGES

beyond
my glacial pace

waits an infinite
well of

love as luscious as butter cream icing
awareness dawning like the sun stretching each morn
wonder as surprising as a sprout from a shriveled stump
passion like crimson tailfeathers dancing for a date

ready to melt
mental ice blocks

Elizabeth Onyeabor

LAP LESSONS

a lady's ride slow
a butcher's ride fast
his legs my pony
me, a wee lass

potbellied gallops
clatter packed pencils
cheer-dappled cheeks
grant stubbled nuzzles

deft, steely fingers
'neath wavy, white mane
"Shoes untied, Daddy"
lacing he trains

ADVENTURELAND

clacking, clacking, clacking
crests

dropping, dropping, dropping
depths

clutching my breath
white knuckling life's lap bar

letting go with a scream
to crush the clouds

and laughter
to summon the sun

Elizabeth Onyeabor

ESCAPING THE SHADOWS

mental murkiness patrols
round and round
detaining me in despair

I shuffle sideways left and right
but stumble again and again
over manacles in my mind

lurking behind each memory
angry throngs assign and accuse
blame, stupidity
judgments my own making

distractions while chambered
deliver temporary reprieves, not acquittals
but shame's shackles keep me captive

rhythm and meter rush to rescue
crushing my uncreative curse
pleading with poetic license

a pilgrimage to pacify
the ever-present swarm
sucking the life from me

the only way is through

embracing a paradox for healing:
releasing requires revisiting
with the same painful intensity

Escaping the Shadows

expressing, sharing sorrows
testifying of my motherly imperfections
his charred arm, her homicidal sitter,
his plummet to the stairwell bottom
until guilt makes way for mercy

facing my shadow self
huddled in our childhood closet
grieving the innocence and white panties
he stole beside his walnut-brown armoire
until fear makes way for love
and by
forgiving

I find
freedom

Elizabeth Onyeabor

EXCITEMENT

wrapped in
silky ribbons and shiny bows

packaged with
surprise and love

KNOWING

the more
I know

the more
I realize

I don't know

and
the more

I want
to know

Elizabeth Onyeabor

MINDFUL

future and past flutter by
what if I fail?
what if I was wrong?

below my shoulder blade
a knot
tenses into steely talons

focus on now

I don't know how

notice, don't ignore, the clawing
hanging on my inhale
falling with my exhale

again and again and again
filling the ribcage
letting it glide

until soft air sings
hmmmm saaaaaah
again and again and again

and talons turn into wings

NEVER

never wander from your path
before traversing its height
what you deem arduous and steep
becomes the most
comforting vantage point
adorned in daisies' merciful meadows

never walk so fast along your path
that you cannot smell which flower
tickles your nostrils with fragrance
or which bird calls to mate
or which parting in the pathway
continues your calling

Elizabeth Onyeabor

RAINBOW RESONANCE

white whispers darling
and plucks heart strings
with the harp

yellow tweets a
canary's mating call
with the flute

orange soars a sweet refrain
jazzing it up
with the saxophone

red sizzles and strikes
orgasmic ecstasy
with the cymbal

blue serenades
blossoming love
with the violin

purple pulses
majestic keynotes
with the grand piano

black bows
silent knowing
with the conductor

WARRING HEART

thump pump
freezing
paralyzing blue

thump pump
thawing
warming red

ready, set, go
battling bloodlines

cobalt cold
shoots dread
immobile

crimson cheer
fires kindled
assurance

drumming rhythms
crested streaming

vanquish
routing throes

triumph
winning freedom

Elizabeth Onyeabor

SUNFLOWERS

she chews on pure joy
cracking and spitting out
shells of black pretense

nutty remnants
seed aftermath's glow

stems of natural splendor
bask in warm knowing

bedding delight
florets sway and nod
to her dazzling future

SEEDS OF LOVE

shimmering golden showers
absorbing sunlit embraces
dancing furry dandelions
spreading eager seeds
floating dainty florets
connecting strewn concerns
opening wholehearted cares
sprouting inner sparkles

Elizabeth Onyeabor

APPRECIATION

the state of appreciation flows
running through my mind's meandering
and the open-hearted passage of intuition
until what I want I block

afraid . . . not worthy

return to appreciation without expectation

melt . . . into joy

emotion runs regardless of what is now

happy, elated, content

water courses through the dam without effort

pours through unguarded channels to the next place
over and over as the brook widens, expands
now a stream
now an ocean

different currents, waves to carry and traverse
each one special yet the same
surfs to slap against or swim amongst
all for learning how to welcome the now
float in foamy cresting till the next surge

IN THE MOMENT

crossing the bridge
feel the breeze
cool my body

fishing boat rocks
empty at anchor
but not ashore

I'm in the moment

sun descending, glowing
a sparkling watery pathway
golden rays parting ways

I'm in the moment

clouds fluffy-white mixed
with purple-gray-pink
painting heaven's landscape
silhouetted shapes and trees

I'm in the moment

joyful jet skiers crisscross
the lagoon's pillared bridge
streaming fountains high

I'm in the moment

pacing with my stride
chest rising lowering to

Elizabeth Onyeabor

my imaginary metronome
trusty shepherd by my side
panting matching gaits
as if no chain holds sway

I'm in the moment

EFFORTLESSLY

what if
it happens
beautifully
easily
and
effortlessly?

this future that
I can't see

why worry
needlessly?

what if
I put faith
into play
leading the way
inspiring my day?

wouldn't that be a
better foray
than to dwell
in dismay?

what if
I focus
on my role
make a goal
within my control?

Elizabeth Onyeabor

act on what's
stirred by my soul
not obsess
on the whole

what if
it happens
beautifully
easily
and
effortlessly?

GO GO GO

go go go
flow flow flow
much as you like
no wrong to write

go go go
wherever you wish
swish like a fish

go go go
soar like a dolphin
make waves and
curly ques

go go go
play in a creative sea
whether pods or schools
never a chore for you

go go go
flow flow flow
pursue
the passion
in you

Elizabeth Onyeabor

NO MORE RUNNING

I run from a skeletal hand
straining to bury me
in unabated bygones
I run from myself
pretending jagged edges
don't nettle my way

inner conflict litters
a trail of dusty tears

I stumble trip fall
to a pounding earth
swallowing all senses

as I kick within its chasm
rocky bottoms offer footing

I step toward angelic arms
advancing a cascade
of compassionate caresses
I dance toward an authentic me
emerging along gentle love's
forgiveness footpath

CONNECTED AGAIN

jade leaves swaying,
in wind's gentle puffs

branches bending, shaking
from monkeys' moving poses
jumping limb to limb

croook, eet eet, birds chirping
others add their own tunes
to the feathery choir
sounds delight my ears

another lands intent on nibbling
insects around lily blossoms
graceful steps on each pad
walking on water floating in air

a swish in the pond
quickly look hoping
to catch a mangrove
mudskipper glimpse
murky water reveals nothing

ascend a ladder
to the trunk's topmost lookout
parallel to monkeys I peek
at nature's green grandeur
a conservation enclave

Elizabeth Onyeabor

what welcome respite
from concreted chaos
eighteen million strong

present with nature past
and connected again

FLOW

when we flow
we go
more than we know
let go

Elizabeth Onyeabor

POTENTIAL

I cradle my bundle of potential

yet untapped, pristine

what will you grow to be?

CLEANSING SOUL

pit of hell
a fiery spit of tale
with fits and starts
sizzle and fizzle
burn of a cleansing soul

sputtered passion sparking
emerging from the flame
pierced by regrets
shielded by misery
warped by forgery
inner discourse fanning

embers searing, sealing
truths of false-flagged irony
black night's armored shroud
forged in steely will
a platinum heaven

Elizabeth Onyeabor

DEPTH DECISION

raging rapids beat against
my frothed anxiety
baring abysmal
thoughts and fears

mental recesses restrain
gush guarded eddies
submerged, you struggle for breath
drown and die in my depths

stillness of soul
sink into healing power
not scary surges
in me cleanse and revive
await to welcome ashore

bridge the current
past stormy seas
my tender tides
awash with mercy

surrender to my flow or
thrash against my squall
whether healing or horrific
you choose

IMPRISONED

wrought-iron window
keeps them out
as long as I remain
a prisoner on the inside

free to leave anytime
of my choosing
if I don't care
about padlocked intent

doors always bolted
whether house or car
self or other
a prisoner on the inside

free to wander anytime
of my choosing
if I don't care
about confronting fears

shifts in perspective
puzzling patterns unfetter
a new me emerging from
a prisoner on the inside

Elizabeth Onyeabor

BREATHING LIFE

wet, warm sand
toes tilling

small, shallow wells
resplendent, naked nucleus

throbbing, rich rhythm
synchronizing the whispering wind

beating together
inhaling the humid heaven

rising, falling
harmonious frothy foam

toes tickling
trickling running away

HEARTFELT HEALING

"Within its womb"

STARLIGHT

a wish upon this
star so bright

a hope to find
my guiding light

a ghastly hand
snuffs your candle's glow

and bedecks in blues
of a deathly foe

though daytime pretends
everything's fine

a screeching specter
retches vile my mind

when will you shine
me a new way

and banish that banshee
whether night or day

Elizabeth Onyeabor

RIVER FLOW

below bank's edge
polychromatic pebbles pool
lining the riverbed
where fish sail within the shallows

upstream, gurgles greet me
foamy tufts misty
waves thump mid-air chest bumps
swift swells down, down stream

naked roots dangle drinking
washed of sand and dirt
primed to nourish and grow

emerald leaves sway and sieve
the sun's noon surge subdued
still power streams unfiltered
from the cerulean sky

self-inflicted hibernation subsides
gratitude washes over winter's freeze
in the sunshine of my summer

reflections of my fluid form
life's boulders but a brief impasse
finding my way onward regardless
though unsure the destination

Escaping the Shadows

what does it matter?

river of life retires to a lake
one day it evaporates
returns as rain and
continues course

Elizabeth Onyeabor

MOTHER PROTECTOR

where were you, mother,
when I lay on the golden velvet bedspread
and the boy in indigo bikini briefs
nearly plucked my red flower skirt?

where were you, mother,
when the man pinned me like a puppet
on the motley braided rug
and sewed my lips shut?

where was I, her mother,
when sobs like a siren
signaled the Pollyanna pretense
of her lethal sitter?

where was I, his mother,
when he tumbled like a weed
past the open basement door
stair after stair after stair to smash on the ground?

where was I, his mother,
when he slid into scalding oil
and fried his arm crispy
like a charred chicken wing?

when will I, mother
of the child within
and the children without,
be enough?

WATERY WONDERS

my mouth foams without anger
fleeing and flowing where 'ere I go

my delicate lace traverses
tittering toes on a beachy sand

my fury rages rock-bottom
damning demons contest your soul

my calm silence shimmers
reflecting who you are or want to be

my secluded shoals offer a warm embrace
bathing in sunshine and wavy arms

my darkest chasm nurtures
healing within its womb

Elizabeth Onyeabor

THINKING IN INK

undertows dredge up
caches of sunken memories
unlocking
silver-lined insights

ebbing, then
evaporating

snaking rivers
through the futile and fallow fields'
outer banks

gentle wind friend
breezes through past flusters
and sails through the current

waving and
beckoning

strokes steer
them all
into ink
the way I think

PENNED FLIGHT

floating fancies

soaring to the stratosphere
or plunging in the crevasse

plumes never perching
hatched from a paper nest

Elizabeth Onyeabor

HEART'S DESIRE

do what you
want to do

dreams really do
come true

heart's desire

work on them
day by day

till they become
your play

light your fire!

MUSICAL MOVEMENT

music moves me
beating rhythmic electricity
lightening my limbs
shifting my cerebellum side to side
a private audience of
mirror and me

stepping shuffling sliding
as I will
where the instrument plays me
sashay and shimmy
that last measure
exploding inside
notational energy

Elizabeth Onyeabor

INNER UNIVERSE

start, finish
never ending

again, spiraling
inner universe

growing, expanding
eternally

AGELESS

coarse curls claim her crown
crow's feet nest round her lids
marionette lines tug at her mouth
a turkey wattle droops about her neck
a trellis crisscrosses her limbs
as superficial sagging
but
ethereal gems gleam from her crown
blue-green insights twinkle 'neath her lids
touching tales pour from her mouth
a vibrant voice resonates from her neck
a budding radiance rises from her limbs
in a spiritual splendor

Elizabeth Onyeabor

O'ER-RUNNETH

filled with compassion
coaching and writing
each day offering
blissful expression
presents of sharing
healing

my cup o'er-runneth

meditation muse
divine inspiring
satiating soul
infinite loving
ever expanding
growing

my cup o'er-runneth

heavenly beauty
thrill beyond measure
or expectation
trusting the current
courses leeward my
learning

my cup o'er-runneth

guiding
stories of anguish

Escaping the Shadows

and shame, then feeling
soothing releasing
filling spaces with
delighting

my cup o'er-runneth

I feel happiness
through habits of joy
pouring to them
the practiced nectar of
nurturing

my cup o'er-runneth

sharing bounty
of abysmal passage
stroking past struggles
self-strength surfacing
drink the eternal
fulfilling

their cups o'er-runneth

Elizabeth Onyeabor

SPRINGTIME SPROUTS

wintery fear wanes
agony abates
ennui subsides
shame slumbers

past fades
gloom brightens
palette paints
springtime sprouts

pleasure emerges
vitality grows
joy blossoms
hope renews

CHRYSALIS

heaviness holds her like a black hole's gravity
sucking each breath in her struggle
to escape through a too-small slit

the membrane cracks just enough to
squeeze one part now another through
thirsty lungs slurp the succulent sky

feeling lighter but lacking
spindly little legs strain to support
raised hands curse the blue beyond
but glisten turquoise gold with unfolding wings

Elizabeth Onyeabor

RESURRECTION

the gray of day
had come my way

snuffed the light
n'er to burn bright

felt in the gloom
forever my doom

till a shift in plight
emerged from the night

SOUL SEARCHING

searing sand dunes shifting
no scenic view of soul
dried in nameless furor
where devils whip and whirl

seeking an oasis
a slake for thirst divine
savior of haboobic hell
baptized badlands mine

Elizabeth Onyeabor

MY BODY

spirit carrier
fragile egg sac
golden-centered yolk
breathing a luminous core
into existence

sturdy shell
eventual crack
contents spilled
nutrients absorbed
by eager hatchlings

ALIGNMENT

feeling great
when I
meditate

to align
with my
inner divine

and I know
in the end
it will all work out
just fine

when I allow
angels to fly
freein' my mind

Elizabeth Onyeabor

TRAUMATIC GROWTH

crackle, sizzle, hiss
laying waste to vibrant blossoms
smoky figments scorn and scourge
scorching every shade in its sweep

nourished in a nursery of new growth
ashes kindle budding insights
blazing vigor both marvelous and minute
coo, sing, hum

FEAR VERSUS LOVE

fear seizes my solar plexus
contracts
burdens
suffocates
in panicked beats

love fills my heart
expands
embraces
warms
in comfortable rhythms

Elizabeth Onyeabor

SOUL SISTER

dreams future and past
bathed in hope and -less
she waters tandem tears and joy
soul sister of mine

revealing shadowy thoughts
lurking in hidden rooms
she knows this specter too
soul sister of mine

keys unlocking potential
lie in camouflaged pieces
she links her own puzzle
soul sister of mine

insights and awareness
intuitive blurts emerging
she taps her own within
soul sister of mine

parallel paths intersect
on this life's journey
she reaches out at will
soul sister of mine

connecting between us
not to feel judging
not to feel shaming
soul sister of mine

Escaping the Shadows

loving in imperfection
as I am, accepting
as she is, accepting
soul sister of mine

Elizabeth Onyeabor

FAMILY PRAYER

keep you near
when not here

in my heart
we never part

blessed be
you
me
and family

SOULMATE DANCE

soulmates entwine
in tremendous tangoes
partnered
with jive jumps and spicy salsas

clap away past missteps
spin with love unconditioned
rhumba into new routines
with our inner divine leading

Elizabeth Onyeabor

SOLITUDE

sensing expanding peace
glowing golden globe

radiant resplendent retreating

burning anxious edges
savoring this moment

GREAT DAY

today's gonna be a great day
today's gonna be a great day
today's gonna be a great day
'cause I'm choosin' that way

no matter what they do or say
I will step from the fray
learn from bumps along the way
'cause my mindset's at play

and that's why you'll hear me say
today's gonna be a great day
today's gonna be a great day
'cause I'm choosin' that way

fears, concerns will hold no sway
toxic self-talk will I slay
my self-care keeps 'em at bay
'cause my mindset's at play

and that's why you'll hear me say
today's gonna be a great day
today's gonna be a great day
'cause I'm choosin' that way

life's no longer blue and gray
sun shines throughout the day
come what may, love leads the way
'cause my mindset's at play

Elizabeth Onyeabor

givin' thanks while I drift away
today was a pretty great day
today was a pretty great day
'cause I chose that way

I CALL MYSELF

I call myself, Elizabeth.
I am in the middle,
embracing Love's hand on my left
beginning our unknown journey

harnessing harmony of opposites,
accepting Fear's hand on my right
I am in the middle.
I call myself, Surrender

Elizabeth Onyeabor

CONTENTMENT

charming trinkets dangling
jingling within reach

ever-flowing chalice
pacifying fears

mother nature's bosom
nursing tender cares

rock-a-bye my child self
readying for rest

nurtured in the rising
sensing of our worth

cherished sparkling treasure
opening within

lullaby's contentment
singing in my soul

SERENITY

I am shimmering rays calming your concerns
I am silken ribbons unraveling your regrets
I am gentle whispers quieting your mind
I am earthen mantles soothing your core
I am tender embers kindling your passion
I am tranquil fields blossoming your blessings
I am still waters nurturing your flow
I am everlasting serenity satiating your soul

Elizabeth Onyeabor

SEVEN LIFE LESSONS

this is my story
of self-discovery
it started out sad
but ended up glad

I wanted to die
and I'll tell you why
my mind told me lies
made me agonize

tried not to get mad
believed it was bad
in complete irony
turned that anger on me

this is my story
of hiding misery
it started out sad
but ended up glad

though a public me
acted cheerfully
private guilt and shame
played a wicked game

maybe like you
wanted to do
something so true
but only saw blue

Escaping the Shadows

this is my story
of painful recovery
it started out sad
but ended up glad

I'd buried my passion
a child's repression
my neighbor's aggression
panties in his possession

learned seven life lessons
to dive in the deep ends
then started to see
a very new me
this is my story
of promise and glory
it started out sad
but ended up glad

what a surprise
a gift in disguise
that through depression
found my expression

came out of my cave
the day I forgave
it wasn't for "he"
I set myself free

this is my story
of self-victory
it started out sad
but ended up glad

Elizabeth Onyeabor

ABOUT THE AUTHOR

Coach, poet, and award-winning, best-selling author Elizabeth Onyeabor loves sharing stories of hope and healing. Deeply drawn to expand self-love's light within us all, she founded the Habitual Happiness Hub. As Chief Ease of Excellence Officer, she coaches and inspires people around the world ready to embrace their whole selves, create lasting joy, and live their dreams.

Elizabeth is the proud mother of three grown children. A transplant from sunny Arizona, she now basks in the shimmering sub-Saharan sun with her beloved husband.

Read More

From the Shadows: A Journey of Self-Discovery and Renewal
The Light Within: Freedom Through Forgiveness

Gifts

Download your gifts at www.ElizabethOnyeabor.com/gifts, including the free ebook, *3 Keys to Feel Good Enough: A 30-Day Guide for a More Joyful You.*

Work with Me

Book a discovery session with me. Let's explore your needs and how to live your dreams.

www.habitualhappinesshub.com/hhhcalendar

Connect with Me

 ElizabethOnyeaborAuthor
 elizabethonyeabor
 efonyeabor

INDEX OF POEMS

Absence, 23
Adventureland, 67
Ageless, 105
Alignment, 113
Am I Worthy?, 27
Amore, 14
Angels and Demons, 54
Appreciation, 78
Argumental, 30
A Shadowy Friend, 52
Bed of Thorns, 19
Belated Grief, 55
Beloved, 13
Bliss Amiss, 47
Blockages, 65
Breathing Life, 92
Breezing, 6
Bullish Surrender, 60
Buts, 28
Caged Bird, 49
Chrysalis, 109
Cleansing Soul, 89
Cockled Bluebells, 41
Connected Again, 85
Contentment, 124
Depression, 25
Depth Decision, 90
Digital Delight, 5

Diving, 59
Dolphin and Dove, 9
Doomed, 38
Effortlessly, 81
Entwining, 15
Escaping the Shadows, 68
Excitement, 70
Expandable, 16
Faces, 50
Failure, 58
Family Prayer, 118
Fear Versus Love, 115
Flow, 87
God's Handiwork, 8
Go Go Go, 83
Great Day, 121
Growth Cycle, 64
Heart's Desire, 102
I Call Myself, 123
Imprisoned, 91
Indecision, 51
Inner Universe, 104
In the Moment, 79
Is It Fear?, 31
Knotted Necklace, 37
Knowing, 71
Lap Lessons, 66
Maybe, 29

Meandering Mind, 24
Mindful, 72
Mother Protector, 98
Musical Movement, 103
My Body, 112
Never, 73
No More Running, 84
O'er-runneth, 106
Pathways, 46
Penned Flight, 101
Persnickity Passion, 17
Poison, 20
Potential, 88
Rainbow Resonance, 74
Remembering You, 22
Resurrection, 110
River Flow, 96
Seeds of Love, 77
Serenity, 125
Seven Life Lessons, 126
Shaming Tree, 44
Shattered, 42
Skiing, 63
Smarts, 21
Solitude, 120
Soulmate Dance, 119
Soul Searching, 111
Soul Sister, 116
Springtime Sprouts, 108
Starlight, 95
Stormed, 34
Sunflowers, 76
Technology Will Not, 7

The Secret, 39
Thief, 57
Thinking in Ink, 100
Timeless, 33
Touching Tempos, 11
Traumatic Growth, 114
Void, 18
Vulnerability, 48
Warring Heart, 75
Watery Wonders, 99
Who Am I?, 53

www.ingramcontent.com/pod-product-compliance
Lightning Source LLC
Chambersburg PA
CBHW022323080526
44577CB00005BA/91